mason jar lunches

50 Pretty, Portable Packed Lunches

Jessica Harlan
photographs by Kelley Klein

Ulysses Press

Published by:
Ulysses Press
P.O. Box 3440
Berkeley, CA 94703
www.ulyssespress.com

ISBN: 978-1-61243-759-0
Library of Congress Catalog Number 2017952133

Printed in Canada by Marquis Book Printing
10 9 8 7 6 5 4 3 2 1

Acquisitions editor: Bridget Thoreson
Managing editor: Claire Chun
Editor: Shayna Keyles
Proofreader: Renee Rutledge
Layout: Jake Flaherty

Distributed by Publishers Group West

table of contents

introduction

Mason jars are fairly ubiquitous these days. Fancy restaurants serve cocktails in them, Pinterest is teeming with craft projects that transform them into everything from light fixtures to glitter-encrusted vases, and product designers are taking inspiration from their iconic shape.

Originally created in 1858 by John Landis Mason as a way for homemakers to preserve the bounty of their gardens safely and reliably, mason jars have been rediscovered by today's home cooks. They've found that these jars are just as handy for fresh foods as they are for canning jams or pickles.

Indeed, these glass jars, with their two-part metal lids, are ideal vessels for creating, storing, transporting, and even serving self-contained meals. Whether prepping a feast for a concert in the park, toting a lunch to the office, or packing a lunch box for school, mason jars can do it all.

One of the biggest producers of glass canning jars, Ball Canning, has been around since 1880. Ball® Brand Fresh Preserving Products are now made by Newell Brands, and the company is capitalizing on the resurgence in popularity of these jars with an expanded range of sizes, shapes, and even accessories. Ball® jars range in size from 4-ounce jars, which

can hold an afternoon snack, to half-gallon vessels ideal for brewing a batch of sun tea. Many companies are even making accessories for the jars: plastic lids, sipper tops, neoprene sleeves that insulate the contents, and infusers to make tea or cold-brew coffee.

In this book, America's favorite container will be put to good use as a stylish and functional container for your lunches and other meals. With a small collection of these jars, you'll be able to pack and transport delicious preparations both hot and cold, from salads to soups to all-in-one bowls.

Why Mason Jars?

There are plenty of reasons why mason jars make the perfect lunch container—here are the top ten:

1. They're inexpensive. A set of two pint-sized (16-ounce) mason jars can be purchased for under $10.

2. They're readily available. You can find canning jars at supermarkets, kitchenware stores, discount stores, or online. You can even find vintage jars at flea markets and antique stores.

3. They're easy to clean. Glass does not stain or retain flavors or odors, and it's dishwasher safe!

4. They're safe. People who are worried about storing food in plastic can rest easy with mason jars. Glass is an inert substance, so it will not leach chemicals into food, even when heated.

5. They're environmentally friendly. Unless it breaks, a glass jar can be used for ages without deteriorating. And when you're finished with it, it can be recycled easily. In fact, glass can be recycled an infinite number of times without losing its quality.

6. They're practical. Glass mason jars can be refrigerated, frozen, or microwaved, although they can crack if subjected to sudden changes in temperature.

7. They're portable. A pint-sized jar, which is the right size for most of the recipes in this book, is only about 5 inches tall and 3½ inches wide. It's easy enough to pack into a purse or a backpack. If you're worried about it breaking, wrap it in a tea towel, which can double as a place mat at your desk.

8. They're versatile. Mason jars are perfect for containing any sort of food, from cook-in-the-jar oatmeal to salad to dessert. And extra jars can be used for many more purposes than packing lunch. In my house, I use mason jars as drinking glasses, toothbrush holders, mini planters, pencil holders, and more.

9. They're great for storage. Glass jars are good for storing foods in the refrigerator or pantry, particularly since they're airtight and watertight. They'll hold the layers of a salad or composed meal intact, and because they're clear, you can easily see what's inside. You can even use a dry-erase marker to label them on the side or the lid.

10. They're trendy. Thanks to their versatility coupled with their retro design, mason jars are quickly becoming iconic. So pat yourself on the back—you are right on the cutting edge!

Your Mason Jar Kitchen

Creating an inventory of tools for making mason jar lunches is easy and inexpensive—you might already have many of these items in your kitchen! Here is a list of the tools I used to create these recipes:

Mason jars: The recipes in this book use either pint jars (16 ounces/2 cups) or half-pint jars (8 ounces/1 cup). I recommend having a set of four each of these sizes. Choose the wide-mouth jar shapes, which are easiest for filling, emptying meals into a bowl, and cleaning. Mini 4-ounce jars are also handy for shaking small amounts of dressings.

Lids: Mason jars come with metal two-part lids: A flat disk with a rubbery edge is the lid, and a threaded ring screws onto a molded thread on the top edge of jar, sealing the lid into place. If they rust or you lose one of the parts, you can buy more lids separately at any place that sells canning supplies. If the two-part lids are annoying to keep track of, you can buy reusable one-piece plastic or metal jar lids.

Small tongs: A set of tongs is convenient for arranging items in the jar.

Small spring whisk: These whisks, with a spiral-shaped wire, are excellent for emulsifying vinaigrettes and other dressings. The base of the spiral is flat, which means you can whisk right in a jar or another flat-bottomed vessel. You can also mix dressings in a half-pint or 4-ounce mason jar. Just put the ingredients inside, screw on the lid tightly, and shake vigorously.

Mason Jar Math

Mason jars are labeled with the imperial volume measurement system, using the old-fashioned culinary terms of pint and half-pint. Here's how those measurements figure in other terms:

1 pint = 16 ounces = 2 cups

1 half-pint = 8 ounces = 1 cup

Kettle: An electric kettle heats quickly to cook recipes like oatmeal and soup, but a stovetop kettle also works. I like kettles with a long spout, like the Bonavita brand kettles used for pour over coffee, because it's easy to direct the stream of water right into the jar.

Small colander: Because many of these recipes only use small quantities of fruit or produce, a mini colander is a useful tool. The company Chef's Planet makes a measuring colander that is ideal for rinsing a handful of berries or cherry tomatoes.

Immersion blender: An immersion blender, or stick blender, is ideal for blending small batches of items, like single-serve smoothies or sauces. It can be used in a small bowl, or come with a special blending cup. But if you don't have an immersion blender, a regular countertop blender works just fine, too.

Mason Jar Lunch Tips

Throughout this book, you'll find detailed instructions for making packed lunches in your mason jars. These tips will help you find success with these recipes or your own creations.

Layer your ingredients.

- **Pint jars hold 16 ounces (2 cups).** They are a good size for a meal like a salad (see Chapter 2), a bowl (see Chapter 4), or a soup base to which water gets added. Smaller, half-pint jars hold 8 ounces (1 cup) and are good for rich desserts, soups, dips, smaller portions, or breakfast-type recipes like oatmeal.
- **Layer your ingredients.** Layering the components of a recipe into the jar not only looks nice, but it can also help keep flavors distinct and the textures of the ingredients fresh. Saucy or liquid ingredients are best on the bottom, while dry or crisp ingredients, such as lettuce, are best on top.

- **Pair a liquid ingredient with a sturdy one.** If there's a dressing or a sauce, place that in the bottom first, and layer a sturdy ingredient on top of it. Meat or crisp vegetables that won't wilt if in contact with liquid are good options. When you empty the jar onto a bowl or plate, the sauce will be on the top of your meal.

- **Utilize waxed or parchment paper or plastic wrap.** A small piece of waxed paper, parchment paper, or even plastic wrap can help separate ingredients that need to stay dry and crunchy, like crackers or breadcrumbs. You can wrap these ingredients in the paper, or you can use the paper to make a "bowl" in the top of the jar for these items, letting the edge stick out of the jar and then screwing the lid over it.

- **Be careful with warm lunches.** If you're adding hot water or other liquids to your meal, make sure the jar and its contents are at room temperature. Otherwise, the shock of the temperature change could cause the glass to crack.

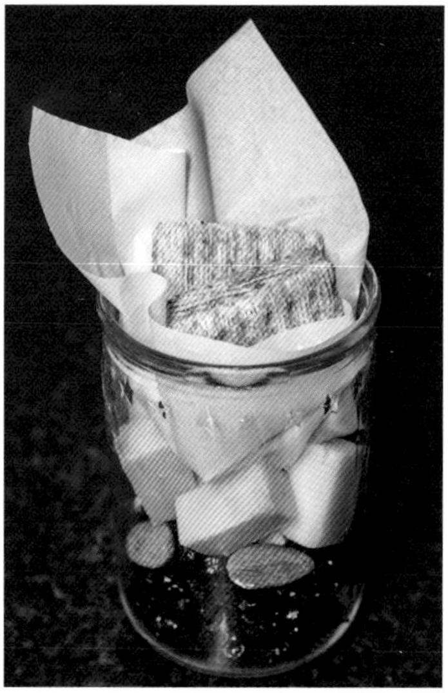

Utilize waxed or parchment paper or plastic wrap.

chapter 1

breakfast for lunch

Sometimes, nothing satisfies a craving quite like the sweet and savory flavors of breakfast foods: rich eggs, hearty oats, sweet maple and cinnamon, and fresh fruits. Why limit these flavors to the morning? The recipes in this section are all satisfying, portable treats that can be enjoyed long past sunrise. Try them for lunch, dinner, or even as evening snacks!

date and almond quick oats

Instant oatmeal is so convenient—just add hot water! But I've always found it to be too sweet, and some of the varieties have a cloying, artificial flavor. Making your own allows you to decrease the sweetness…or increase it (no judgment here!). Be sure to use oats labeled instant oats or quick oats; they've been precooked, dried, and rolled out thinner than traditional rolled oats, so they soften quickly.

JAR SIZE: half pint   MAKES: 1 serving

½ cup quick oats
3 pitted dried dates, chopped
1 tablespoon powdered milk
1 teaspoon dark brown sugar
1 tablespoon sliced almonds
¼ teaspoon cinnamon
¾ cup boiling water

1. To assemble the jar, layer half of the oats, half the chopped dates, the remaining oats, the powdered milk, the brown sugar, and then the remaining dates. Add a layer of almonds, then sprinkle cinnamon on top. Jars can be assembled and stored at room temperature, tightly covered, for up to a week.

2. To prepare, fill the jar to the top with boiling water, using a spoon to stir the water in. Let sit, loosely covered, for 3 minutes until the oats are softened and creamy. Eat straight from the jar or spoon into a bowl.

Note: I used dried dates for their richness and chewy texture, but you can peruse the dried fruit section of your supermarket's bulk-food aisle for other options. Dried cherries, cranberries, blueberries, apples, or figs would all be tasty additions. You can also use maple sugar in place of the brown sugar.

layered yogurt parfait

This easy and satisfying meal is a good grab-and-go breakfast or afternoon snack. Choose a super-crunchy granola (and watch out—some granola varieties are very high in fat and calories!), which will keep from getting too mushy from the yogurt and the juice of the fruit.

JAR SIZE: half pint   MAKES: 2 servings

6 ounces plain or vanilla Greek yogurt

⅔ cup assorted berries or diced stone fruit

⅔ cup granola

2 teaspoons honey

1. In two half-pint jars, divide the yogurt, berries or stone fruit, and granola. If desired, create two layers of each ingredient.

2. Drizzle a teaspoon of honey over the top. Refrigerate for up to 2 days and eat chilled.

Note: The thicker consistency of Greek yogurt helps keep the layers separate, and it also doesn't make the granola as soggy if it's made ahead of time, but you could also use regular yogurt in a pinch. The fruit, honey, and granola add sweetness naturally, but if you have a sweet tooth, try vanilla- or coconut-flavored yogurt.

MASON

tropical coconut chia pudding

You might associate chia with the 1970s grassy-haired fad product, Chia Pets. But today, it's the latest superfood, a tiny black seed from the desert plant *Salvia hispanica*. Chia is rich in omega-3 fatty acids, fiber, protein, and antioxidants, and when it's added to a liquid, it thickens that liquid into a pudding-like consistency. For this recipe, use a refrigerated variety of coconut milk rather than the thick type that comes from a can.

JAR SIZE: half pint   MAKES: 1 serving

½ cup coconut milk

2 tablespoons plus 2 teaspoons chia seeds

½ teaspoon vanilla extract

1 teaspoon maple syrup

1 tablespoon coconut flakes

¼ cup diced fresh tropical fruit like pineapple, mango, or kiwi

1. Place the coconut milk in a small mixing bowl. Sprinkle the chia seeds into the milk and stir to combine. Stir in the vanilla and maple syrup.

2. Transfer the mixture to a half-pint jar, scraping up any stray seeds. The mixture will not completely fill the jar. Cover and refrigerate for 4 hours or overnight.

3. After the pudding has thickened, toast the coconut flakes in a small, nonstick skillet. Toast over medium-high heat, stirring frequently, until the coconut has turned lightly golden, 2 to 3 minutes.

4. Transfer the coconut to a small plate or bowl, and let cool. Spoon the tropical fruit over the chia pudding and sprinkle the coconut on top. The pudding will keep, covered and refrigerated, up to 3 days.

Note: If possible, give this pudding a stir a couple of times as it's setting. This will help distribute the seeds and prevent them from settling on the bottom, which creates a gummy layer in the bottom of the jar.

raspberry-chocolate smoothie jar

I didn't understand what the fuss was about smoothie bowls until I finally tried one: Thick, creamy, and icy cold, it was like eating ice cream with (healthy, of course!) sprinkles on top for breakfast! Keep chunks of fruit in the freezer so you'll be able to make one of these jars at a moment's notice. An immersion blender and a blending cup are just the right size to blend up a single serving. And although I've chosen the combination of dark chocolate, berries, and toasted walnuts, you can choose your own delicious toppings. Granola, dried fruit, a drizzle of honey…the choice is yours.

JAR SIZE: half pint MAKES: 1 serving

6 ounces vanilla Greek yogurt

½ medium banana, cut into chunks and frozen

¼ cup frozen raspberries

⅛ cup fresh raspberries

1 tablespoon toasted walnuts

1 tablespoon chopped dark chocolate

1. Using a countertop blender or an immersion blender with a bowl or blending cup, add the yogurt, banana, and frozen raspberries. Blend until smooth, occasionally using a small spatula to stir chunks up from the bottom of the blending cup or bowl. The smoothie will be very thick and spoonable, like soft-serve ice cream.

2. Spoon the mixture into the jar. Top with fresh raspberries, then walnuts, then chocolate.

breakfast salad with grapefruit vinaigrette

Buttered toast, tangy grapefruit, a perfectly cooked egg, and, of course, crispy bacon. They're all here in this salad, which is as delicious at lunchtime (or even dinner!) as it is in the morning.

JAR SIZE: pint MAKES: 2 servings

2 eggs
3 slices bacon
1 medium pink grapefruit
½ teaspoon honey
⅛ teaspoon kosher salt, or more to taste
2 tablespoons extra-virgin olive oil
1 medium red pepper, cut into strips
1 cup baby spinach
1 cup croutons (see page 22)
freshly ground black pepper, to taste

1. Place the eggs in a small saucepan and cover with cool water. Bring to a boil, reduce heat to medium-low to maintain a simmer, and cook for 3 minutes. Turn off the heat, remove the eggs, and transfer to a small bowl filled with ice water. Set aside. When cool, peel the eggs but leave them whole. This method makes an egg where the yolk is set but still just the tiniest bit runny.

2. In a medium nonstick skillet, cook bacon over medium heat until crisp, turning occasionally, 4 to 5 minutes. Transfer the cooked bacon to a paper towel–lined plate and set aside.

3. Supreme the grapefruit (see page 22), reserving the juice. Squeeze the center membranes of the grapefruit into a bowl. Discard the membrane.

4. In a small bowl or jar, whisk together 2 tablespoons of the reserved grapefruit juice with the honey, salt, and pepper. Whisk in the extra-virgin olive oil. Set aside.

5. To assemble the jars, divide the vinaigrette between two pint jars. In layers, add the red pepper, grapefruit sections, spinach, and croutons. Crumble the bacon over the croutons. Slice the eggs in half and nestle them on top. Salad will keep, covered and refrigerated, for up to 1 day.

How to supreme citrus: To *supreme* is the technique of segmenting a citrus fruit while removing the skin and the tough membranes. It's a valuable technique to master for making professional-looking fruit salads, garnishes, and other dishes. Here's how:

Slice off the top (stem end) and bottom of the grapefruit, just enough to expose the meat of the fruit. Using a paring knife or utility knife, carefully slice the rind off in strips, following the curve of the fruit. Holding the peeled fruit in one hand and working over a bowl to catch the juices, cut along the membrane of one section on both sides to make a V-shaped notch. Use the knife to flick the cut section of the fruit into the bowl. Repeat with each remaining section.

croutons

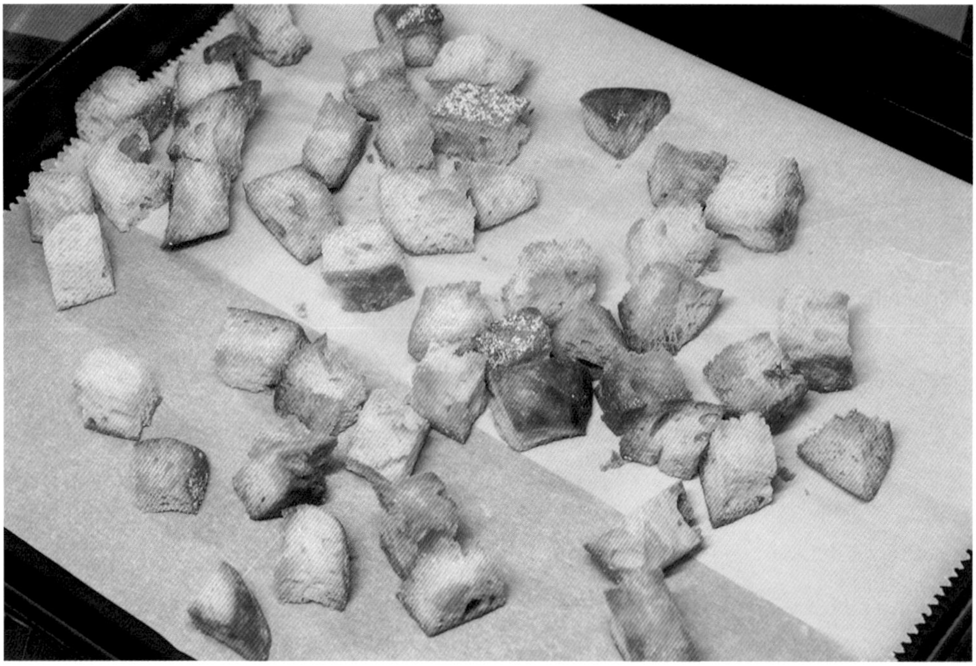

If you have one, a toaster oven is just the right size to prepare a batch of these crunchy bites, which can add interest to any salad. You can use a baguette instead of sliced bread for this recipe.

MAKES: 2 cups

2 cups sliced white bread cut into ¾-inch cubes, crusts removed
2 tablespoons extra-virgin olive oil or melted unsalted butter
pinch kosher salt

1. Preheat the oven to 350°F.

2. Place the cubed bread in a bowl, drizzle with the olive oil or butter, and toss to coat the bread bits.

3. Spread onto a baking sheet and sprinkle lightly with salt. Cook for 10 to 15 minutes, stirring and turning every 5 minutes, until golden and crisp.

4. Cool completely and store in a zip-top bag for up to 3 days. Croutons can also be frozen, in a bag, for up to a month. Defrost at room temperature and crisp in a 350°F oven for 2 to 3 minutes before using.

chapter 2

layered salads

With their crisp, colorful ingredients arranged in a rainbow of layers, mason jar salads are a fun and easy lunch. They're practical, too: By putting the dressing on the bottom and layering ingredients so that the dressing won't make croutons or other more delicate components soggy, your salad will travel well and be fresh and appealing when you're ready to eat. On the following pages, I've translated some favorite salads into mason jar lunches and given you some new ideas, too!

caprese salad

Cherry tomatoes and ciliegine (fresh mozzarella formed into small balls) are just the right shape and size for a mason jar salad. The balsamic vinaigrette, with its balance of sweet and tangy, is a nice accent to the creamy mozzarella and the spicy basil. Pair this with a crusty baguette or a bowl of tomato soup.

JAR SIZE: pint MAKES: 1 serving

½ teaspoon Dijon mustard
2 tablespoons balsamic vinegar
⅛ teaspoon kosher salt
3 tablespoons extra-virgin olive oil
1 cup halved cherry tomatoes
¼ cup whole basil leaves
½ cup halved ciliegine mozzarella
freshly ground black pepper, to taste

1. In a small mixing bowl, whisk together the mustard, vinegar, salt, and black pepper until smooth. While whisking, drizzle in the olive oil. Season to taste with more salt and pepper as needed.

2. Pour the dressing into the bottom of a 16-ounce jar. In layers, add the tomatoes, then the basil, and then the mozzarella balls. Refrigerate until you are ready to eat, up to 1 day.

3. To serve, pour into a shallow bowl and toss to distribute the ingredients and dressing.

provençal salad

This salad channels the south of France, with its herby dressing, capers, olives, and imported tuna. It keeps for a few days, so it's a good salad to make on the weekend for a mid-week lunch. Use good-quality tuna, packed in oil or spring water and sea salt, for the best texture and flavor. I'm a fan of the Genova Tonno brand.

JAR SIZE: pint   MAKES: 2 servings

1 tablespoon plus ⅛ teaspoon kosher salt, divided

¾ pound (4 to 6) baby red potatoes

½ pound green beans, trimmed

2 eggs

1 teaspoon Dijon mustard

2 tablespoons Champagne vinegar

1 teaspoon dried herbes de Provence

2 turns freshly ground black pepper

3 tablespoons extra-virgin olive oil

1 can premium tuna, packed in oil, drained

1 tablespoon capers

2 tablespoons pitted Kalamata olives, sliced or chopped

1. Bring a small saucepan of water to a boil and add 1 tablespoon salt. Prepare a bowl of ice water.

2. Add the potatoes to the boiling water and cook for 5 minutes. Add the green beans and cook for 5 minutes more, until potatoes are tender when pierced and beans are crisp-tender.

3. With a slotted spoon, remove the vegetables and shock in ice water to cool them quickly.

4. Return the water to a boil, add the eggs, cover, and remove from heat. Let stand for 12 minutes.

5. Remove the eggs and rinse them under cool water. Let sit until cool enough to touch, then peel the eggs and cut each into four wedges.

6. While the eggs are cooking, make the dressing by whisking together the mustard, vinegar, herbes de Provence, remaining salt, and pepper. While whisking, drizzle in the olive oil, and set aside.

7. When the vegetables are cool enough to touch, separate the potatoes from the green beans, and cut them into bite-sized halves or quarters. Cut the green beans into 1-inch pieces. In a small bowl, combine the tuna, capers, and olives.

8. To assemble, divide the dressing between two pint jars. Layer in the potatoes, green beans, tuna mixture, and eggs. Cover and refrigerate until needed, up to 2 days. To serve, turn the salad out into a bowl or plate.

fruit salad with citrus dressing

Make a jar or two of these refreshing salads at the beginning of the week, and you'll be grateful you did. Cool and refreshing, they're just the right pick-me-up for a mid-afternoon snack or a light breakfast. Pair it with a whole-grain muffin or a yogurt for more substance. I like to combine traditional and tropical fruits, as used in this recipe, but you can use whatever fruit looks good at the market...anything goes!

JAR SIZE: pint MAKES: 1 serving

2 tablespoons fresh orange juice, from half an orange

2 teaspoons lime juice, from 1 lime

2 teaspoons honey

½ cup honeydew melon balls

½ cup halved strawberries

½ cup fresh pineapple chunks

½ cup canned mandarin oranges, drained

2 tablespoons sweetened coconut

1. In a small bowl, whisk together the orange juice, lime juice, and honey until the honey has dissolved into the juice.

2. Pour the dressing into the bottom of a pint jar. Layer the melon, strawberries, pineapple, and oranges into the jar, sprinkling coconut in between each layer as desired. Cover and refrigerate until needed.

3. To serve, invert the jar to let the dressing coat the fruit. Open the lid and pour into a bowl, or eat straight from the jar.

Note: A melon baller is an inexpensive gadget, and it will transform the honeydew quickly into bite-sized balls. You can get a ratcheting pineapple cutter to easily cut the pineapple, or do it with a chef's knife, like this: Cut the stem and the base off the pineapple and place it upright on a cutting board. Cut off the rind from top to bottom in thick slices. Cut the pineapple in half vertically, then cut each half into long, wedge-shaped segments. Cut off the inner edge of each segment to remove the core. Then slice each wedge into chunks.

1 CUP

deconstructed shrimp caesar

Caesar salads are ubiquitous on restaurant menus for a reason: The combination of crunchy croutons, crisp Romaine lettuce, earthy Parmesan, and creamy dressing is simply irresistible. Add a protein, as I've done with a few perfectly sautéed shrimp, and it becomes a satisfying meal. You can also use a few slices of grilled chicken or chunks of seared or grilled salmon instead of shrimp in this main-course salad.

JAR SIZE: pint MAKES: 1 serving

3 ounces large shrimp, peeled and deveined

3 tablespoons extra-virgin olive oil, divided

1 teaspoon grated lemon zest

¼ teaspoon black pepper, plus more to taste

¼ teaspoon kosher salt, plus more to taste

2 tablespoons plain Greek-style yogurt

1 tablespoon lemon juice

½ teaspoon anchovy paste

¼ teaspoon garlic powder

dash Worcestershire sauce

1 cup shredded romaine lettuce

¼ cup croutons (see page 22)

2 tablespoons grated Parmesan cheese

1. Place the shrimp in a small bowl, and drizzle with 1 tablespoon of olive oil. Toss to coat. Sprinkle the shrimp with the lemon zest, black pepper, and kosher salt, and toss to distribute the seasonings.

2. Heat a medium nonstick skillet over high heat and add the shrimp. Sauté for 3 to 4 minutes, turning occasionally with tongs, until the shrimp is pink and opaque. Remove to a plate, and set aside. If the salad is to be stored, cool and chill the shrimp in the refrigerator.

3. In a small bowl, make the dressing by whisking together the yogurt, lemon juice, anchovy paste, garlic powder, and Worcestershire sauce. While whisking, drizzle in the remaining 2 tablespoons of olive oil. Season to taste with salt and pepper.

4. To assemble the salad, pour the dressing into the bottom of a 16-ounce mason jar. Layer in half the romaine, half of the cooled shrimp, the remaining romaine, and the remaining shrimp. Place the croutons on the top and sprinkle with the Parmesan cheese.

5. Refrigerate until you are ready to eat, up to 2 days. To serve, pour into a shallow bowl and toss to distribute the ingredients and dressing.

buffalo chicken salad

I created this salad for my husband, who loves buffalo chicken wings. Just like the game-day snack, the spiciness of the chicken is nicely tempered with a creamy blue cheese dressing and crisp celery. Best of all, it's not nearly as messy as gnawing on a chicken wing!

JAR SIZE: pint MAKES: 2 servings

10 ounces chicken breast meat, cut into chunks

⅛ teaspoon black pepper, plus more as needed, divided

1 tablespoon butter

2 teaspoons vegetable oil

¼ cup hot sauce, such as Frank's Red Hot

2 tablespoons mayonnaise

2 tablespoons sour cream

1 tablespoon white wine vinegar

3 tablespoons blue cheese crumbles, divided

dash Worcestershire sauce

1 cup shredded iceberg lettuce

2 ribs celery, thinly sliced into crescents

kosher salt, to taste

1. Season the chicken with salt and pepper to taste. In a medium nonstick skillet, over medium heat, melt the butter and oil together until hot. Add the chicken and cook, turning pieces occasionally with tongs, for 2 minutes or until the chicken is just beginning to brown.

2. Add the hot sauce and continue to cook over medium-low heat for 5 more minutes, stirring and turning occasionally, until the chicken is cooked through. The internal temperature should be 165°F when checked with a meat thermometer. Remove from heat and transfer to a plate or a bowl.

3. While the chicken is cooking, make the dressing. In a small bowl, combine the mayonnaise, sour cream, and vinegar, and stir until smooth. Stir in 2 tablespoons blue cheese, Worcestershire sauce, and the remaining ⅛ teaspoon black pepper.

4. To assemble, pour the dressing into the bottom of the jar. Add the lettuce, then the chicken, then the celery. Top with the remaining 1 tablespoon blue cheese crumbles.

beet, pistachio, and orange salad with goat cheese

This salad is a beauty to behold with its vibrant orange wedges and ruby-red beets. Look for cooked, peeled beets in the produce section of your supermarket—it's way easier than cooking them, and the texture is better than canned or jarred beets. When you supreme the oranges (see the instructions on page 22), be sure to reserve the juice for the dressing.

JAR SIZE: pint MAKES: 1 serving

¼ teaspoon Dijon mustard
2 tablespoons freshly squeezed orange juice
1 tablespoon red wine vinegar
⅛ teaspoon kosher salt
2 turns freshly ground black pepper
2 tablespoons extra-virgin olive oil
¾ cup cooked beets, cut into ½-inch cubes
1 orange, sectioned
1 cup mixed salad greens
2 tablespoons crumbled goat cheese
2 tablespoons shelled pistachios

1. In a small bowl, whisk together the mustard, orange juice, and vinegar. Whisk in salt and pepper. While whisking, add the olive oil gradually.

2. To assemble, pour the dressing into the bottom of a pint jar. Layer in the beets, orange segments, greens, goat cheese, and pistachios. Refrigerate, covered, until needed, up to 2 days.

Note: To cook beets for this salad, trim the root and stem from two to three medium raw beets, then cut them lengthwise into quarters, unpeeled. Place a steamer basket in a medium pot with about an inch of water beneath. When the water simmers, place the beets in the basket and steam, covered, for 15 to 20 minutes or until they are tender when pierced with a fork. Let cool, then rub the peel off with a paper towel. It should slip off fairly easily.

southern-style chicken salad

When I took an informal poll of my Southern girlfriends, it seemed like everyone had a different —and strong!—opinion of what goes into a proper chicken salad. Some add hard-boiled egg, some say that's sacrilege. Some add celery, some don't. Grapes are an occasional ingredient, as is Vidalia onion. Most agree that Duke's brand mayonnaise is crucial. Since the opinions differed so wildly about what constitutes a good Southern chicken salad, I had to come up with my own favorite combination of ingredients. And so can you.

JAR SIZE: half pint   MAKES: 2 servings

8 ounces cooked chicken breast, diced

3 tablespoons dried cranberries

2 tablespoons toasted diced pecans

2 ribs celery, diced

2 tablespoons mayonnaise, or more as needed

½ teaspoon dried tarragon

⅛ teaspoon kosher salt

2 turns freshly ground black pepper

2 leaves butter lettuce

2 croissants, for serving

1. In a bowl, combine the chicken, cranberries, pecans, and celery. Stir in the mayonnaise until it coats the ingredients evenly. Sprinkle with the tarragon, salt, and pepper, and stir to distribute.

2. To assemble, spoon the chicken into two half-pint jars. Fold the lettuce and stuff it into the top of the jar. Cover and refrigerate until needed, up to 2 days. To serve, pack split croissants separately, and make a sandwich with the lettuce and salad.

Note: While you can buy precooked chicken at the supermarket or use leftovers from a roast, you can also buy a raw chicken breast and poach it. Simply submerge it in water or, better yet, chicken or vegetable broth. Feel free to add aromatic ingredients, like a slice of onion, some crushed garlic cloves, a pinch of dried herbs, or a few stems of fresh herbs. Bring the liquid to a simmer, then reduce to low and cook, covered, for 15 to 18 minutes until the chicken measures an internal temperature of 160°F. Remove from the poaching liquid and let cool.

chapter 3

noodles and pastas

Hot or cold, Italian or Asian or Americanized, pasta has universal appeal. In the following recipes, it takes on various forms in layered jars, some of which are meant to be heated, some of which can be enjoyed cool or room temperature. I've aimed to include colorful garnishes and ingredients in these recipes so that they're as pretty as they are delicious. And because most of the recipes make two servings, they're ideal for lunch *au deux*.

pesto penne and chicken

Use jarred pesto from the supermarket or make your own using basil from your garden for this recipe, which pairs pesto-coated noodles with grilled chicken breasts and yellow squash. It is an ideal dish to make in the summer, when both basil and yellow squash are at their peak and plentiful.

JAR SIZE: pint MAKES: 2 servings

10 ounces boneless, skinless chicken breast

1 teaspoon kosher salt, divided

1 teaspoon freshly ground black pepper, divided

2 yellow squash, quartered lengthwise

1 tablespoon extra-virgin olive oil

1 tablespoon vegetable oil

lemon wedge

4 ounces penne

2 tablespoons prepared pesto

1. Place chicken breasts between two sheets of waxed paper. Using a meat mallet or the bottom of a heavy pan, pound chicken to about ¾-inch thickness. Season the chicken with ½ teaspoon salt and ½ teaspoon pepper.

2. Drizzle the squash with olive oil and season with the remaining salt and pepper.

3. Heat a grill pan or a grill to medium-high heat. Brush the grill grates with vegetable oil, then cook the chicken and squash for 9 to 11 minutes, turning the squash occasionally to grill sides evenly, and turning the chicken over after 5 minutes. The squash should be softened, with grill marks, and the chicken should be 165°F when measured with a meat thermometer.

4. Remove chicken and squash from the grill, transfer to a plate, and immediately squeeze the lemon over the chicken and the squash. Let cool.

5. While the chicken and squash are cooking, cook the penne according to package directions. Drain, place in a bowl, and immediately toss the hot pasta with the pesto, stirring to coat the pasta evenly. To assemble, layer the squash, chicken, and penne in two pint jars.

tortellini with herby vinaigrette, olives, and roasted red peppers

Fresh tortellini from the supermarket refrigerator case makes a quick foundation for this layered pasta salad recipe. With its briny olives and roasted red peppers, it has the flavors of an Italian charcuterie platter. You could add diced salami to make it even more substantial, experiment with different filled tortellini flavors, or even use mini ravioli.

JAR SIZE: pint MAKES: 1 serving

1 cup tortellini, fresh or dry

3 tablespoons extra-virgin olive oil, divided

½ teaspoon grainy Dijon mustard

2 tablespoons white wine vinegar

½ teaspoon dried thyme

½ teaspoon dried tarragon

⅛ teaspoon kosher salt

⅛ teaspoon freshly ground black pepper

½ cup sliced roasted red peppers

½ cup halved and pitted Kalamata olives

1. Cook tortellini in boiling water according to package directions. Drain and rinse well under running water until cooled completely. Place in a bowl and toss with 1 tablespoon olive oil to prevent pasta from sticking. Set aside.

2. In a small bowl, combine grainy mustard, vinegar, thyme, tarragon, and salt and pepper. Whisk to combine. While whisking, drizzle in the remaining 2 tablespoons olive oil, and whisk until the mixture is emulsified.

3. To assemble, pour the dressing into the bottom of a 16-ounce mason jar. Alternate adding layers of the pasta, the roasted peppers, and the Kalamata olives, ending with the peppers and olives on top. Refrigerate, covered, until ready to serve, up to 2 days.

Note: To roast your own peppers for this recipe, place a whole red bell pepper directly onto a gas burner or on a heated grill. Use tongs to turn the pepper as the side closest to the heat source blackens and blisters. Continue to turn and roast until the majority of the pepper is blackened, 7 to 10 minutes total. Immediately transfer the pepper to a small bowl and cover it tightly with plastic wrap. Let rest until the pepper is cool enough to handle. Using your hands or a dry paper towel, rub the blackened skin away from the pepper (try rubbing under running water to make this easier). Then cut pepper flesh into strips. Roasted pepper can be mixed with olive oil and stored, covered, in the refrigerator for 2 weeks, or frozen in plastic bags for up to 3 months.

CUP

soba noodles with ginger dressing, iceberg lettuce, and tofu

This Japanese take on a chilled noodle salad uses soba noodles, which are made from buckwheat flour and have a delicately nutty flavor and a firm texture. This recipe uses baked tofu, which you can usually find in the produce or natural foods refrigerated section of your grocery store. You can use plain tofu, but for more flavor, look for marinated versions, such as teriyaki, sesame ginger, or Thai spice.

JAR SIZE: pint MAKES: 2 servings

6 ounces soba noodles

1 teaspoon minced ginger

2 tablespoons rice vinegar

2 teaspoons honey

⅛ teaspoon kosher salt

1 teaspoon sesame oil

2 tablespoons vegetable oil

1 (6-ounce) package baked tofu, cut into bite-sized chunks

2 carrots, peeled and grated

1 cup shredded iceberg lettuce

1. Cook soba noodles in boiling water according to directions. Drain into a colander and rinse well under cool water until the noodles have cooled.

2. In a medium bowl, whisk together the ginger, rice vinegar, honey, and salt. While whisking, drizzle in the sesame and vegetable oils.

3. Add the cooled noodles to the bowl and toss to coat the noodles evenly with the dressing.

4. Assemble by layering two pint jars with the tofu, noodles, carrots, and lettuce. Pour any remaining dressing into the jars. Serve chilled or at room temperature. The jar will keep, covered and refrigerated, for up to 3 days.

peanut noodles with cucumber and red pepper

There was a time in my life when I'd get peanut noodles delivered at least once a week from my local Chinese restaurant. I loved the richness of the sauce, the chewy noodles, and the fresh, crisp contrast of a garnish of scallion or cucumber. Although the sauce has a lengthy list of ingredients, most of them are staples you probably have at home, and it's completely worth it for the complex flavors of sweet and salty, tangy and creamy.

JAR SIZE: pint MAKES: 2 servings

6 ounces angel hair pasta

1 teaspoon sesame oil

1 clove garlic, minced

¼ teaspoon red chile paste

2 teaspoons soy sauce

1 tablespoon lime juice

1 teaspoon brown sugar

2 tablespoons creamy peanut butter

1 tablespoon hot water

2 teaspoons toasted sesame seeds, plus more for garnish

½ cucumber, peeled, seeded, and thinly sliced into half-moons

red bell pepper, sliced into thin, 1-inch matchsticks

2 tablespoons chopped fresh cilantro

1. In a pot of boiling water, cook the angel hair pasta according to package directions. Drain in a colander.

2. While the pasta is cooking, make the sauce. In a medium bowl, combine the sesame oil, minced garlic, chile paste, soy sauce, lime juice, brown sugar, and peanut butter. Stir in the hot water until the sauce is smooth and creamy.

3. Add the drained pasta to the bowl of sauce while still hot and use tongs to toss the noodles, coating them completely with the sauce. Stir in the sesame seeds.

4. To assemble, divide the noodles between two jars. Top with the cucumber, bell pepper, cilantro, and additional sesame seeds. Serve at room temperature or chilled.

Ball

pasta with sausage and broccoli rabe

Have you ever eaten a meal that you remember—and try to replicate—for years? For me, it was a simple pasta dish at an Italian restaurant in Chicago that I tasted maybe 25 years ago. It was a simple dish: a short pasta with hearty sausage, bitter greens, spicy red pepper flakes, and earthy Parmesan cheese. It was just a perfect combination, and one that I've tried to recreate ever since. This layered mason jar dish comes pretty close, and tastes good both warm and cold.

JAR SIZE: pint MAKES: 2 servings

1½ cups gemelli or other short pasta

1 tablespoon extra-virgin olive oil

¼ teaspoon red pepper flakes

¼ teaspoon kosher salt, plus more to taste

2 spicy sausage links, raw, casings removed

2 cloves garlic, minced

3 cups (about 4 ounces) broccoli rabe, chopped

2 tablespoons Parmesan cheese

1. In salted, boiling water, cook pasta according to package directions. Drain and transfer to a bowl. Drizzle with the olive oil and sprinkle with red pepper and salt. Toss to combine.

2. While the pasta is cooking, in a large skillet, over medium-high heat, sauté the sausage, breaking it up into small chunks, until browned and cooked through, 6 to 8 minutes. Add the garlic and cook, stirring constantly, for 30 seconds or until lightly browned. Add the broccoli rabe and cook until leaves are wilted, 2 to 3 minutes. Remove from heat.

3. To assemble, create layers with the pasta and the broccoli rabe–sausage mixture. Sprinkle with the Parmesan cheese. Refrigerate until needed, up to 3 days. To serve, microwave the jar for 1 minute or more, until heated through. Turn out into a shallow bowl.

lasagna in a jar

Using round ravioli, just the right size to fit into a half-pint mason jar, is a good cheat for making lasagna. This recipe layers the ravioli with all the other lasagna fixings: marinara sauce, ricotta cheese, and mozzarella. If you are a meat lover, you can brown 4 to 6 ounces of ground beef or turkey and add it to the layers.

JAR SIZE: half pint MAKES: 2 servings

8 ounces round, fresh ravioli
1 tablespoon olive oil
½ cup ricotta cheese
2 tablespoons Parmesan cheese
½ teaspoon Italian seasoning
3 turns freshly ground black pepper
1 cup prepared marinara sauce
4 ounces grated mozzarella cheese

1. Cook ravioli according to package directions, drain, and rinse. Transfer to a bowl and drizzle with olive oil to prevent sticking. Set aside.

2. In a small bowl, combine the ricotta cheese, Parmesan, Italian seasoning, and black pepper.

3. To create the jars, spoon about a tablespoon of sauce into the bottom of each jar. Layer with ravioli, a spoonful of ricotta, a spoonful of sauce, and a tablespoon of mozzarella. Make as many layers as will fit, ending with the mozzarella. You will likely have extra ingredients.

4. Refrigerate until needed, up to 3 days. To serve, set on a microwaveable plate and microwave uncovered for 1½ minutes until cheese melts and the pasta is heated through. Turn out into a bowl.

Note: For variation, try different types of ravioli fillings, such as spinach, mushroom, or artichoke. You can also use pesto instead of the marinara sauce for a summery version.

blt pasta

If there's a BLT on the menu, there's a 99 percent chance I'm going to order it, no matter what the other options are! So I couldn't resist using the components I love most about BLTs in a chilled pasta dish that's just as crisp and refreshing as the sandwich.

JAR SIZE: pint MAKES: 2 servings

⅛ teaspoon kosher salt, plus more to taste

1½ cups dry fusilli noodles

4 slices thick-cut bacon, cut crosswise into ¼-inch strips

¼ cup mayonnaise

¼ cup buttermilk

1½ tablespoons cider vinegar

1 teaspoon minced fresh dill

½ teaspoon garlic powder

2 turns freshly ground black pepper

⅔ cup shredded iceberg lettuce, divided

1 cup halved cherry tomatoes, divided

1. Bring a medium pot of salted water to a boil. Cook noodles according to package directions, until al dente. Drain, rinse with cool water, and transfer to a small mixing bowl, then set aside.

2. Meanwhile, in a medium nonstick skillet, cook the bacon over medium heat until crisp, about 7 to 9 minutes. With a slotted spoon, transfer to a paper towel–lined plate, and set aside.

3. To make the dressing, in a small bowl, whisk together the mayonnaise, buttermilk, vinegar, dill, and garlic powder. Season with the remaining ⅛ teaspoon salt and pepper. Pour the dressing over the pasta and toss to coat.

4. To assemble the jars, divide the pasta between two jars. Layer half the bacon over the pasta in each jar, followed with ⅓ cup lettuce and ½ cup tomatoes in each. Refrigerate until ready to serve, up to 1 day. To serve, pour into bowls and toss to combine the ingredients.

zoodles with creamy avocado sauce

While I tend to think that zoodles ("noodles" created from spiral-cut zucchini or other vegetables) aren't fooling anyone, they do have their place in my meal rotation. Rather than trying to imitate pasta, I prefer to give them their own treatment with a luxurious sauce that tastes decadent but is actually fairly healthy, since it's made with avocado and yogurt.

JAR SIZE: pint MAKES: 2 servings

1 pound (2 medium) zucchini

1 tablespoon plus ½ teaspoon kosher salt, divided

1 avocado

6 ounces plain Greek yogurt

½ lime, juiced

½ teaspoon garlic powder

2 tablespoons pumpkin seeds

1 tablespoon chopped cilantro

1. With a spiralizer or a vegetable peeler, cut zucchini into noodles or ribbons. Set the zucchini noodles into a colander in the sink and sprinkle with 1 tablespoon salt. Use your hands to toss the noodles to distribute the salt. Let drain for 10 to 15 minutes, then pat the noodles as dry as possible with paper towels. This removes excess water from the noodles and keeps them firm.

2. While the noodles are draining, scoop the avocado into a countertop blender or small bowl, if you will be using an immersion blender. Add the yogurt, lime, garlic powder, and the remaining ½ teaspoon salt, and blend until creamy.

3. Divide the noodles between two pint jars and spoon the sauce over. Garnish with pumpkin seeds and cilantro. Refrigerate until needed, up to 1 day. To serve, eat straight from the jar or turn out onto a plate and toss to combine.

Note: A spiralizer is a kitchen gadget that looks a bit like a pencil sharpener but has toothed blades to shred vegetables like zucchini or cucumbers into long, ribbon-like strands. They're fairly inexpensive and you can find them in the kitchenware department of most stores.

chapter 4

bowls in a jar

A complete meal packed into one compact jar? The recipes in this section are all hearty, substantial meals, good for lunch or dinner. Take them on a road trip, pack them with an ice pack for a long bike ride, or stash them in your desk drawer. They'll satisfy even the biggest appetite.

farro and roasted vegetable bowl

Farro is an ancient Mediterranean wheat variety that's just now becoming recognized in the United States. When cooked, it has a wonderfully chewy texture and a nutty flavor. It is high in fiber, complex carbohydrates, and magnesium. Unless you want to be watching your pot for an hour or more, be sure to look for quick-cooking, or pearled, farro, which has part of the hull removed. You'll trade a bit of that nutrition for convenience, however; pearled farro is lower in fiber.

JAR SIZE: pint MAKES: 2 servings

2 cups trimmed, halved Brussels sprouts

2 cups cauliflower florets

1 red onion, sliced

4 tablespoons extra-virgin olive oil, divided

¾ teaspoon kosher salt, divided

6 turns freshly ground black pepper, divided

1 cup quick-cook farro

2 teaspoons butter

¼ cup panko breadcrumbs

1 teaspoon grainy Dijon mustard

2 tablespoons white wine vinegar

1. Preheat the oven to 400°F. Spread the Brussels sprouts, cauliflower, and red onion on a parchment-lined baking sheet (keep them separate if you want to layer them individually). Drizzle with 2 tablespoons olive oil and sprinkle with ½ teaspoon salt and 3 turns pepper. Roast for 15 to 20 minutes, until browned.

2. While the vegetables are roasting, cook the farro as directed on the package. Drain excess water. Transfer to a mixing bowl and let cool.

3. In a small skillet, melt the butter. Add the breadcrumbs and toast, stirring frequently, until the breadcrumbs are browned. Transfer to a plate.

4. In a small bowl, whisk together the mustard, vinegar, the remaining ¼ teaspoon salt, and 3 turns pepper for the dressing. While whisking, drizzle in the remaining olive oil.

5. To assemble, divide the dressing between two pint jars. Layer in the Brussels sprouts, farro, cauliflower, and onion. Sprinkle with the breadcrumbs.

poke sushi bowl

Poke shops (pronounced POH-keh) are popping up everywhere, and for good reason! Poke bowls combine marinated raw fish, a Hawaiian specialty, with cooked rice and a variety of toppings and sauces. Use a wide-mouth jar for this recipe.

JAR SIZE: pint MAKES: 2 servings

1 cup short grain white rice, such as Nishiki sushi rice

1 tablespoon rice vinegar

½ teaspoon kosher salt

2 tablespoons ponzu sauce

1 teaspoon sesame oil

1 teaspoon sesame seeds

½ teaspoon minced ginger

1 cup (about 6 ounces) raw salmon filet, cut into ¾-inch chunks

1 medium avocado, diced

⅔ cup diced, peeled cucumber

½ cup strips of nori or seaweed snack

1. Place the rice in a medium saucepan and rinse by filling the pan halfway with water, rubbing handfuls of the rice between your fingers, then pouring off the water, catching stray grains with your cupped hand. Repeat the rinsing process two or three times until the water is nearly clear. Drain as much water as possible, then add 2 cups of water. Heat the saucepan over high heat, uncovered, until it comes to a boil. Reduce heat to as low as possible, cover, and let cook for 15 minutes.

2. Remove the rice from the heat and let stand, covered, for 10 minutes. Fluff the rice with a fork. Sprinkle with the rice vinegar and the salt, and stir with the fork to combine. Set aside, uncovered.

3. In a bowl, whisk together the ponzu sauce, sesame oil, sesame seeds, and ginger.

4. To assemble, divide the sauce equally between two jars. Layer in the salmon, avocado, cucumber, and seaweed, then finish with ½ to ¾ cup rice, lightly packing everything in. Place the lid on the jar. To serve, invert the jar over a plate or shallow bowl and shake to release. You may need to run a knife around the side to loosen. Jars can be prepared several hours before eating, and stored in the refrigerator.

Variation: For a spicier version, mix 2 tablespoons of mayonnaise with 1 tablespoon of Asian chile sauce, such as Sriracha sauce. Use this in place of the ponzu sauce at the bottom of the jar.

Note: Only use the best-quality fish you can find, from a reliable fishmonger. Ideally, it should be packaged as sushi-grade. While not an official, FDA-rated standard, it does mean that the fishmonger has deemed it safe to eat raw. Nervous about eating raw fish? Try using seared and cooled tuna, cooked salmon, or real or imitation crabmeat.

autumn bowl

With rich roasted veggies, hearty kale, chewy barley, and a sage-tinged vinaigrette made with maple syrup and apple cider vinegar, this bowl resonates with the season.

JAR SIZE: pint   MAKES: 2 servings

4 tablespoons extra-virgin olive oil, divided

1 small shallot, minced

1 cup pearled barley

2½ cups water

1½ cups raw butternut squash, cut into ¾-inch cubes

1 cup peeled parsnips, cut into ¾-inch cubes

2 turns freshly ground black pepper, plus more to taste

1 tablespoon maple syrup

2 tablespoons apple cider vinegar

½ teaspoon Dijon mustard

¼ teaspoon dried sage

⅛ teaspoon kosher salt, plus more to taste

2½ cups raw kale, roughly chopped

½ cup dried cranberries

1. Preheat the oven to 400°F. In a medium saucepan, heat 1 tablespoon olive oil over medium heat. Add the shallot and sauté, stirring frequently, until the shallot is softened and translucent, about 5 minutes.

2. Add barley, 2½ cups water, and a pinch of salt to the saucepan. Bring mixture to a simmer over medium-high heat, then reduce heat to medium-low to maintain a simmer. Cover the pan and cook for 25 minutes or until the barley is tender and the water is absorbed. Drain excess water in a colander and let cool.

3. While the barley is cooking, spread the squash and parsnips on a parchment-lined baking sheet. Drizzle with 1 tablespoon olive oil and season lightly with salt and pepper. Toss the vegetables in the pan to coat with oil. Roast for 25 to 30 minutes or until the vegetables are softened and browned. Remove from oven and let cool.

4. In a small bowl, whisk together the maple syrup, apple cider vinegar, mustard, and sage. Season with about ⅛ teaspoon salt and 2 turns black pepper. While whisking, drizzle in the remaining 2 tablespoons olive oil.

5. Place the kale in a medium bowl. Pour about half the maple vinaigrette over the kale. Using clean hands, massage the kale by squeezing handfuls of it and rubbing between your fingers. Continue massaging until the kale is softened and wilted, almost as if it's been sautéed.

6. To assemble the jars, divide the kale between the two pint jars. Layer the barley into the jars, then the roasted vegetables. Drizzle the remaining maple vinaigrette on top and sprinkle with the cranberries. Serve at room temperature or store in the refrigerator for up to 2 days.

300
200

white bean and salmon bowl

Pickled onions are the tangy, brightly hued highlight of this healthy bowl, which is full of protein from the beans and omega-3 fatty acids from the salmon. Although my ingredient list calls for canned salmon for its convenience, it's a good way to use up a bit of leftover cooked salmon filet from a previous night's dinner. Canned tuna would also work.

JAR SIZE: pint   MAKES: 2 servings

1 (15-ounce) can white beans, drained and rinsed

3 tablespoons extra-virgin olive oil, divided

½ teaspoon minced fresh thyme

5 turns freshly ground black pepper, divided

1 (5-ounce) can salmon, drained

2 teaspoons freshly squeezed lemon juice

2 tablespoons pickling liquid (from pickled red onions; see note)

½ teaspoon Dijon mustard

⅛ teaspoon kosher salt

1 cup baby arugula

⅓ cup pickled red onion (see note)

1 tablespoon chopped fresh parsley

1. In a bowl, combine the beans with 1 tablespoon olive oil, fresh thyme, and 3 turns of freshly ground pepper. In another bowl, combine the salmon with the lemon juice.

2. To make the dressing, in a small bowl, combine the pickling liquid, Dijon mustard, salt, and 2 turns of freshly ground pepper. Whisk until smooth. While whisking, drizzle in the remaining 2 tablespoons olive oil, whisking until it is emulsified.

3. To assemble, divide the dressing between 2 pint jars. Layer in the beans, arugula, salmon, and pickled onion. Top with a sprinkling of parsley. To serve, turn the jar out into a shallow bowl or plate and toss to combine.

How to Make Pickled Onions: To make pickled onions, cut a red onion in half. Thinly slice one half into strips and reserve the other half for another use. Place in a small bowl and pour boiling water over the onion to cover. Let sit 30 seconds, then drain in a colander. Pour 1 cup rice vinegar into a pint mason jar, and stir in ¾ teaspoon kosher salt and 1 teaspoon granulated sugar. Add the onions, pushing down to submerge them into the vinegar mixture. Cover and refrigerate for 30 minutes and up to 1 week. Extra pickled onions can be used as a sandwich or burger topping, on salads, or added to pasta, egg, or potato salad.

mediterranean bowl with creamy greek dressing

I tried to combine all my favorite flavors from Greek cuisine into one delicious jar. With grilled chicken, crisp veggies, creamy chickpeas, and tangy feta cheese, I think it's got all the components needed for a picnic by the sea. And, if you happen to be stuck at your desk instead, well, hopefully the creamy lemony dressing will transport you to sunnier climes.

JAR SIZE: pint MAKES: 2 servings

8 ounces boneless, skinless chicken breast

2 teaspoons lemon pepper seasoning or Greek rub

1 tablespoon vegetable oil

1 clove garlic, minced

2 tablespoons lemon juice

½ teaspoon dried oregano

2 tablespoons plain Greek yogurt

2 tablespoons extra-virgin olive oil

⅛ teaspoon kosher salt

2 turns freshly ground black pepper

1 (15-ounce) can chickpeas, drained and rinsed

1 medium red bell pepper, cut into chunks

1 small cucumber, peeled and cut into chunks

2 marinated artichokes, cut into quarters

½ cup pitted Kalamata olives

2 tablespoons crumbled feta cheese

1. Heat a grill or a grill pan to medium-high heat. Place the chicken between two sheets of waxed paper and use a meat mallet or the bottom of a heavy pan to pound it to an even ¾-inch thickness. Season on both sides with the rub or seasoning.

2. Brush the grill grates with vegetable oil, then place the chicken on the grill. Cook for 4 to 5 minutes on each side, turning over once, until grill marks appear and chicken is 165°F when checked internally with a meat thermometer. Remove from the grill and let cool, then slice into strips.

3. To make the dressing, in a small bowl, combine garlic, lemon juice, oregano, and yogurt. While whisking, drizzle in the olive oil until emulsified. Stir in the salt and pepper.

4. To assemble, pour the dressing into two pint jars. Layer in the chickpeas, red pepper, cucumber, chicken, artichokes, Kalamata olives, and feta. Serve cold or at room temperature.

burrito jar

It was a revelation when my local burrito shop started offering all the burrito fixings, but in a bowl rather than on a big tortilla. Not only was it easier to eat, but healthier, too! I realized that the ingredients can fit just as nicely into a jar, to be enjoyed at room temperature or heated. I usually pack a little container of tortilla chips or a soft whole wheat or corn tortilla to eat with this.

JAR SIZE: pint   MAKES: 2 servings

1 package boil-in-a-bag brown rice
½ pound ground turkey
2 teaspoons taco seasoning
1 avocado
1 tablespoon prepared salsa
1 cup pinto beans, drained and rinsed
1 small tomato, diced
½ cup shredded pepper jack cheese

1. Cook brown rice according to package directions. Set aside to cool.

2. In a medium nonstick skillet over medium heat, brown the ground turkey for 5 to 7 minutes, breaking up the big chunks until it is no longer pink. When it is almost finished cooking, sprinkle the taco seasoning over the meat and stir to combine.

3. Scoop the avocado into a small bowl. Add the salsa and stir to combine, mashing the avocado and the salsa together.

4. To assemble, spoon about ½ cup rice into each of two pint jars. Layer the beans, turkey, avocado mixture, tomatoes, and cheese into the jar. Refrigerate until serving, up to 2 days. To serve, turn out into a bowl and eat cool or at room temperature.

Note: If you want to enjoy your burrito bowl hot, then pack the avocado mixture and the tomato separately. Microwave the jar for 1 to 2 minutes, until hot and the cheese is melted, then turn out into a bowl and top with the avocado and tomato.

parmesan quinoa with grilled chicken and arugula

Nutritious quinoa is one of the few plants that is a complete protein. It's also delicious, with a slightly grassy flavor and a texture that pops a little in your mouth. I've added lemon and grilled chicken to make this recipe a bright-tasting, summery meal.

JAR SIZE: pint MAKES: 2 servings

4 teaspoons extra-virgin olive oil, divided

½ medium shallot, minced

½ cup white quinoa

1 cup water

¼ cup grated Parmesan cheese

1 teaspoon kosher salt, divided

6 turns freshly ground black pepper, divided

8 ounces boneless, skinless chicken breasts

2 tablespoons freshly squeezed lemon juice, from 1 lemon

1 teaspoon grainy Dijon mustard

½ teaspoon honey

1½ cups baby arugula

1. Heat 2 teaspoons olive oil in a small saucepan over medium heat. Add the shallot and sauté, stirring frequently, until softened and translucent, 3 to 4 minutes. Add the quinoa and cook, stirring, for 1 minute or until it smells toasty.

2. Add the water. Bring to a simmer then reduce heat to low, cover, and simmer for 10 minutes. Remove from heat and let sit for 5 minutes, until the water is completely absorbed.

3. With a fork, stir in the Parmesan cheese, ¼ teaspoon salt, and 2 turns black pepper. Set aside.

4. Heat a grill pan or an outdoor grill to medium-high heat. Place the chicken between two sheets of waxed paper and use a meat mallet or the bottom of a heavy pan to pound it to an even ¾-inch thickness. Season on both sides with ½ teaspoon salt and 2 turns black pepper. Cook for 4 to 5 minutes on each side, until grill marks appear and the interior temperature is 165°F. Remove from the grill and let cool, then slice into large chunks.

5. In a small bowl, whisk together the lemon juice, mustard, and honey. Season with the remaining ¼ teaspoon salt and a turn or two of black pepper. While whisking, drizzle in the remaining 2 teaspoons olive oil and whisk until the mixture emulsifies.

6. To assemble, divide the dressing between 2 pint jars. Layer in the chicken, arugula, and quinoa. Refrigerate until needed, up to 2 days. To eat, turn out into a shallow bowl or a plate and toss to distribute dressing. Serve cold or at room temperature.

chapter 5

soups

With their twist-tight seal, mason jars are a good vessel for storing and transporting soups. There's also an advantage that the glass is microwave-safe for heating—just make sure that you wrap the jars in a dishtowel or another cloth to protect your hands, because the glass will get hot! I've even seen patterns for knitting a little cozy for a mason jar.

Instead of microwaving, some of these recipes call for hot water to be added to the contents of the jar to create a soup. Make sure that the jar or the ingredients inside aren't cold, because the shock of the temperature change could cause the glass to break. Instead, bring the contents to room temperature first, or transfer them to a bowl and then add the hot water.

ramen with egg and broccoli

My first book, *Ramen to the Rescue*, explored the countless ways one could use those packaged squares of ramen noodles. And when I started working on this book, I instantly thought of the noodles and how quickly they cooked. I designed this recipe to be a better version of those instant noodles that come packed in Styrofoam cups. It's a delicious hot meal that you can even make in an office break room, if you have access to hot water.

JAR SIZE: pint MAKES: 1 serving

1 egg

1 chicken bouillon cube

¼ teaspoon onion powder

¼ teaspoon poultry seasoning

dash ground ginger

1 package instant ramen noodles, seasoning discarded

⅓ cup raw broccoli, cut into small florets

1. Place the egg in a small saucepan and cover with cool water. Bring to a boil, reduce heat to medium, and simmer for 3 minutes. Turn off the heat, remove the egg, and transfer to a small bowl filled with ice water. Set aside. When cool, peel the egg but leave it whole. This method makes an egg where the yolk is set but still just the tiniest bit runny.

2. In a small bowl, crush the chicken bouillon cube and stir in the onion powder, poultry seasoning, and ginger.

3. To assemble, break the noodle cake into big chunks and put into bottom of jar. Sprinkle with the chicken bouillon mixture. Add the broccoli to the jar and top with the egg. Cover and refrigerate for up to 3 days.

4. To serve, bring to room temperature or transfer to a bowl. Pour boiling water into the jar to the top (if making the soup in a bowl, you'll need about 1¼ cups of water). Let sit for 3 minutes. Pour into a bowl and use a knife to slice the egg in half, and place the egg on top of the soup. Serve hot.

fresh tortellini in broth with spinach

Tortellini made with fresh pasta, which is found in the refrigerator case at the supermarket, only takes minutes to cook, and can even be cooked through with the addition of boiling-hot water. This soup is fast to put together and quick to prepare when you're ready to eat. The chicken broth concentrate that the recipe calls for is a thick paste to which you add boiling water to make a broth. Look for it with the soups and broths in your grocery store.

JAR SIZE: pint   MAKES: 2 servings

1 (9-ounce) package fresh tortellini
1½ cups chopped baby spinach leaves
4 teaspoons concentrated chicken broth
½ teaspoon dried oregano

1. In two pint jars, layer the tortellini and spinach. Drizzle two teaspoons of broth concentrate in each jar and sprinkle with the oregano. Cover and refrigerate until needed, up to 3 days.

2. To serve, bring the jar to room temperature or transfer to a bowl. Pour boiling water over the noodles and let sit 3 to 5 minutes, until the tortellini is tender. Stir to combine and eat hot.

creamy cucumber gazpacho

This cool and creamy soup is just the thing for a hot summer evening. Pack it for a picnic, along with a baguette and some cheese, or serve it with a BLT sandwich. It's quick and easy to make—no stove required!

JAR SIZE: half pint   MAKES: 2 servings

¾ pound cucumbers (about 2), peeled, seeded, and cut into chunks

1 cup plain, low-fat yogurt

1 clove garlic, minced

1 tablespoon chopped fresh dill, plus more for garnish

1 tablespoon freshly squeezed lemon juice

½ teaspoon kosher salt

⅛ teaspoon white pepper

1. Using a countertop blender or a bowl and immersion blender, combine the cucumbers, yogurt, garlic, dill, and lemon juice. Blend until the mixture is smooth, with just a few chunks remaining for texture. Season with the salt and pepper.

2. Divide between the two half-pint jars. Garnish with remaining chopped dill. Serve cold.

watermelon gazpacho

This refreshing summer soup couldn't be easier: Just put all the ingredients into a blender and give it a quick buzz. This soup would make a delicious poolside lunch, especially if you pack it with lots of ice so it stays super-cold.

JAR SIZE: half pint   MAKES: 2 servings

2 cups cubed seedless watermelon

½ cup diced red bell pepper

½ cup diced, peeled cucumber

1 tablespoon diced shallot or pickled red onion (see recipe, page 67)

1 teaspoon minced jalapeño (optional)

1 tablespoon red wine vinegar

½ tablespoon extra-virgin olive oil

¼ teaspoon kosher salt

1 tablespoon roasted pumpkin seeds, for garnish

1 tablespoon minced cilantro, for garnish

1. Add the watermelon, bell pepper, cucumber, shallot or onion, and jalapeño to a countertop blender, or use a bowl or blending cup with an immersion blender. Blend until mostly liquefied, but still retaining a little bit of texture. Stir in the vinegar, olive oil, and salt.

2. Pour into two half-pint jars and garnish with pumpkin seeds and cilantro. Keep covered and refrigerated for up to 3 days. Serve chilled.

tomato soup with grilled cheese croutons

This cozy classic is a favorite among my kids (although I pack it in a Thermos rather than a mason jar). If you're used to the canned variety, you might be surprised to discover that this soup is easy to make and tastes so much better.

JAR SIZE: pint or 2 half-pint MAKES: 2 servings

1 tablespoon butter
1 small shallot, minced
1 (15-ounce) can diced tomatoes
1 tablespoon tomato paste
½ cup chicken or vegetable broth
1 tablespoon chopped fresh basil
2 tablespoons heavy cream
⅛ teaspoon kosher salt
2 to 3 turns freshly ground black pepper
2 slices white sandwich bread
1 tablespoon butter
2 slices sharp cheddar cheese

1. In a small saucepan, melt the butter over medium-low heat. Add the shallot and sauté, stirring frequently, until softened and translucent, 2 to 3 minutes. Add the tomatoes, tomato paste, and broth, and bring to a simmer over medium-high heat. Simmer, uncovered, for 10 minutes.

2. Add the basil and remove from the heat. Using a countertop blender or a bowl and an immersion blender, puree until smooth. Stir in the cream, salt, and pepper. Let cool.

3. To make grilled cheese croutons, spread each slice of bread with butter. Sandwich the cheese between the bread, with the buttered sides facing out. Heat a small nonstick skillet over medium heat and cook, flipping over occasionally, until both sides of the bread are toasted and the cheese is melted. Let cool, then cut into quarters.

4. Pour the soup into two half-pint jars or one pint jar. Wrap the croutons in plastic wrap or line the open space in the top of the jar with waxed paper, and nestle croutons into the paper. Cover and store, and transport upright.

5. To serve, heat the soup, uncovered, in a microwave for 30 seconds to a minute until it has reached desired temperature. Pour into a bowl and float two croutons on the soup.

miso udon soup

Udon noodles are thick and chewy wheat noodles, and can be found in the international aisle of a well-stocked supermarket. If you have access to an Asian grocery store that carries fresh udon noodles, use those instead, as their texture is much better.

JAR SIZE: pint   MAKES: 2 servings

1 bundle (2½ ounces) dry udon noodles

4 tablespoons white miso

1 scallion, white and light green parts, thinly sliced

2 ounces dried mushrooms

1 sheet nori, cut into 1-inch strips

1. Heat a small saucepan of water to a boil. Add the noodles and cook for 3 minutes, just until flexible. Drain and rinse with cool water, until the noodles are no longer hot.

2. To assemble the jars, divide the noodles between two pint jars, coiling them as you place them inside. Spoon 2 tablespoons miso over the noodles in each jar. Sprinkle with the scallion, the dried mushrooms, and the nori. Store at room temperature until ready to serve, up to 4 hours.

3. To serve, fill the jars with boiling water. Let sit for 3 minutes, then pour into a bowl, stir to mix ingredients, and eat hot.

chapter 6

spreaders, dippers, and snacks

Sometimes you don't need a substantial lunch, but instead, just a little pick-me-up. That's what this chapter is all about: the snacks and treats that can be enjoyed throughout the day, by yourself or with friends. Stock up on half-pint jars, or, if you can find them, even smaller jars like 6- or 4-ounce sizes, especially the kind that have wide mouths that makes it easy to access the contents. These portable snacks are great for after school, long commutes, road trips, or to serve up at a meeting.

BREAD

capered tuna

I created this riff on tuna salad for my daughters, who love when I pack tuna in their lunch, although I worry about the mayonnaise not being kept cool enough in a stuffy lunchbox. And they like it even better than traditional tuna salad. It is light and tangy and delicious when spooned onto crackers or, as I suggest in the note below, slices of grilled baguette. Use the best-quality canned tuna you can find.

JAR SIZE: half pint or quarter pint MAKES: 1 to 2 servings

1 (5-ounce) can water-packed tuna, drained

1 tablespoon freshly squeezed lemon juice

1 tablespoon extra-virgin olive oil

2 tablespoons capers

2 teaspoons minced fresh parsley

freshly ground pepper, to taste

1. In a bowl, combine the tuna, lemon juice, olive oil, capers, parsley, and pepper. Use a fork to stir to combine.

2. Pack into a half-pint jar or two 4-ounce jars. Refrigerate until needed, up to 3 days. Serve on crackers or with grilled baguette.

Note: To grill toasts to serve with the capered tuna, thinly slice 4 to 6 pieces of baguette. Brush each side with extra-virgin olive oil. Heat a grill pan or an outdoor grill to high heat. Arrange the baguette slices diagonally over the grill grates and grill for 2 to 3 minutes, until the underside is lightly browned and grill marks appear. Turn over and grill 2 to 3 minutes more. Cool completely before wrapping in plastic wrap. Store at room temperature, up to 1 day.

pimento cheese and crackers

There's no need to use fancy cheddar cheese for this favorite Southern appetizer—even the plastic-encased block from the supermarket will suffice, as long as it's extra sharp. As a Southern transplant, I prefer to use Duke's mayonnaise, but any variety of full- or low-fat mayo will do. I like to add in a handful of green olives for a briny kick. You can omit them for a more traditional version.

JAR SIZE: quarter pint MAKES: 2 servings

2 ounces sharp cheddar cheese, freshly grated

1 tablespoon jarred minced pimentos

1 tablespoon minced pimento-stuffed green olives (about 5 whole olives)

2 tablespoons mayonnaise

1 dash hot sauce, such as Tabasco

crackers, to serve

1. In a small bowl, combine the cheese, pimentos, and olives with a fork. Stir in the mayonnaise, using the fork to mash the ingredients together to form a chunky spread. Add the hot sauce to taste, and stir to combine.

2. Pack the dip into two 4-ounce jars, and pack crackers separately. Or, pack the dip into an 8-ounce jar, add a layer of waxed paper to separate, then fill the top half of the jar with round crackers, such as Ritz. Dip will keep for up to a week. Don't pack the crackers until the day you plan to eat the dip.

Note: Be sure to grate the cheddar yourself, rather than buying pre-grated cheese. Grated cheese has a drier texture and a powdery residue (thanks to the anti-clumping ingredient that's added) that won't be as appealing in this dip.

fruit and cheese snack

My supermarket has a wide selection of little plastic snack-to-go trays that are great for when hunger pangs strike while I'm grocery shopping. But it pains me to buy them because I know I could buy the ingredients for much less money. What's more, packing them in reusable jars is so much less wasteful than the plastic containers they come in.

JAR SIZE: half pint or smaller   MAKES: 2 servings

1 ounce roasted almonds

2 ounces hard cheese like cheddar or Grana Padano, cut into cubes

½ cup dried cranberries or apricots

1. To assemble, layer the nuts, cheese, and fruit into half-pint jars. Refrigerate until needed, up to 3 days.

Note: Mix and match the fruits, nuts, and cheese to your preference. Dried fruits could include dates, pineapple, or raisins. Try cashews, walnuts, or pistachios for the nuts. And any hard cheese, such as gouda, Parmesan, or Manchego would be a good option.

honeyed yogurt with fruit spears

This sweet pick-me-up is a welcome treat for kids and adults alike. Apples are the most dippable fruits, but you could also transport chunks of fruit, like strawberries or cantaloupe, and serve them with toothpicks or skewers for dipping.

JAR SIZE: half pint   MAKES: 1 to 2 servings

6 ounces plain Greek yogurt
1 tablespoon honey
1 teaspoon cinnamon
½ teaspoon vanilla extract
green apple wedges, to serve

1. In a small bowl, combine the yogurt, honey, cinnamon, and vanilla extract. Stir well to combine, then transfer to a half-pint jar. If there's room with the lid on, stick the apple wedges into the jar. Otherwise, pack the apples separately.

Note: To prevent browning, dip the apples into a small bowl of water to which the juice of one lemon has been added. The acid of the lemon will help prevent browning. Or, pack the apple whole and bring a knife or an apple wedger to cut the apple just before serving.

charcuterie stack

Pack this little snack, along with a single-serve bottle of wine, a blanket, and a good book, for an afternoon in the park. (It also makes a good mid-afternoon pick-me-up at work…minus the vino, of course!) I like to keep an assortment of different cheeses and sausages in my fridge so that I can assemble one of these jars at a moment's notice. My kids like it for school lunch, too!

JAR SIZE: half pint MAKES: 1 serving

4 thick slices cheese

4 thick slices sausage

4 round or square crackers, such as Ritz or Triscuit

1. To assemble, cut the cheese so it fits inside the jar, about 2 inches long. You can use a metal biscuit cutter, 2 inches in diameter, to cut the cheese into rounds, if desired.

2. Layer the cheese and the sausage into the jar. Add a piece of waxed paper on top of the cheese and sausage, and place the crackers on the waxed paper to prevent them from getting soggy. Refrigerate until you are ready to eat, up to 1 day.

Note: Some good charcuterie combinations include dried chorizo and Manchego cheese; salami and sharp white cheddar; sliced Parmesan and prosciutto (you can fold thin slices of prosciutto to fit into jar); summer sausage and Wensleydale cheese; bresaola and Pecorino Romano; and soppresata and provolone.

"crab" salad with crackers and endive

This decadent little salad reminds me of something a 1950s hostess might have served to her bridge club. I like to serve it with a gin and tonic or an icy-cold martini when we have friends over for dinner. Look for imitation crabmeat—which is made from a combination of fish that's been seasoned—in the seafood department of your supermarket.

JAR SIZE: half pint   MAKES: 2 servings

1 cup imitation crabmeat, chopped
1 rib celery, finely chopped
3 tablespoons mayonnaise
1 tablespoon freshly squeezed lemon juice
⅛ teaspoon kosher salt
2 turns freshly ground black pepper
1 tablespoon minced fresh parsley
endive leaves, for serving (optional)
Ritz crackers, for serving (optional)

1. In a bowl, combine the crabmeat, celery, mayonnaise, lemon juice, salt, pepper, and parsley. Stir to coat the crabmeat and celery in the mayonnaise and lemon.

2. Transfer the mixture to a half-pint jar. Cover and refrigerate until needed, up to 4 days. Serve with endive leaves or Ritz crackers.

herby yogurt dip with crudité

This zesty, creamy dip is super-satisfying for an afternoon slump or to go with sandwiches at a picnic. If you can collect enough tiny jars, individual servings of dip would be adorable in a buffet presentation or at each place setting for a dinner party.

JAR SIZE: quarter pint   MAKES: 4 servings

1 cup plain Greek yogurt (whole or low-fat)

1 tablespoon finely chopped kale

1 tablespoon minced parsley

1 teaspoon minced fresh dill

½ teaspoon garlic powder

⅛ teaspoon kosher salt

vegetables, for serving

1. In a bowl, combine the yogurt, kale, parsley, dill, garlic powder, and salt. Stir well to combine.

2. Divide the dip between the jars, and arrange several vegetable sticks in the jars, with the ends of the vegetables dipping into the yogurt dip. The dip will keep, refrigerated, for up to 1 week—it's actually better if it sits for several hours to a day. Don't prepare or add the vegetables until just before packing or serving.

Note: Peeled carrots, peeled and seeded cucumber, celery, and bell peppers would all be good vegetables to use for this dip. Cut the veggies into thin spears, short enough to fit inside the jar.

dilly onion dip with chips

Anyone who's a fan of the French onion dip found in convenience stores and supermarkets will love this fresh-tasting version that's just the right amount for you and a friend. This dip is good with fresh veggies, but I like to indulge with a stack of Pringles-type potato chips, which just so happen to fit perfectly into an 8-ounce mason jar! As for the dip, a short, wide-mouth half-pint jar is the perfect shape for scooping.

JAR SIZE: quarter pint or half pint   MAKES: 2 servings

⅓ cup light sour cream
2 tablespoons mayonnaise
1 tablespoon dried minced onion
1 teaspoon dried dill
½ teaspoon onion powder
¼ teaspoon kosher salt
dash Worcestershire sauce

1. In a small bowl, combine the sour cream, mayonnaise, dried onion, dill, onion powder, salt, and Worcestershire sauce. Stir well to combine completely.

2. Spoon mixture into 4-ounce jars or 1 wide-mouth half-pint jar, cover, and refrigerate until needed, up to 1 week.

chapter 7

desserts

If you're the type of person who just can't help yourself around sweets, mason jar desserts are a great solution for one reason: portion control. Packed in 4- or 8-ounce jars, these tasty treats are self-contained. And as with salads, the clear glass lends itself to lots of pretty layers of colorful and flavorful ingredients. I'm guessing you won't be able to look through this section without your salivary glands working overtime.

caramelized banana pudding

This recipe, which pairs creamy vanilla pudding with crunchy cookies and gooey caramelized bananas, will sate the most serious sweet tooth. It's a fun dessert that would make a good finale to the BLT Pasta (page 54) or the Buffalo Chicken Salad (page 34).

JAR SIZE: half pint MAKES: 4 servings

1 (3.4-ounce) package instant vanilla pudding mix

1 tablespoon butter

2 tablespoons brown sugar

¼ cup roasted peanuts, plus more for garnish

2 bananas, peeled and sliced into ½-inch pieces

12 Nilla Wafer cookies

1. Prepare the pudding according to package directions, then set aside.

2. In a medium nonstick skillet, combine the butter and brown sugar over medium-low heat. Stir until the butter has melted and the mixture is syrupy. Add the peanuts and stir to coat. Add the banana slices and stir to combine. Simmer over medium-low heat until the bananas are softened. Transfer to a shallow bowl to let cool.

3. To prepare, break the Nilla Wafers into large chunks. Divide between the mason jars; each gets about 3 whole cookies. Spoon the pudding into the jars over the cookies. Spoon the banana mixture over the pudding. Garnish with additional peanuts.

chocolate mug cakes

Mug cakes are genius for those times that you're craving just a little treat, rather than a whole cake. And jars are just as convenient as a coffee mug for cooking up these microwaveable goodies.

JAR SIZE: half pint MAKES: 1 serving

3 tablespoons unsweetened cocoa
2 tablespoons all-purpose flour
1 tablespoon powdered sugar
dash salt
3 tablespoons milk
2 tablespoons melted butter, cooled
¼ teaspoon vanilla extract
1 tablespoon semisweet chocolate chips
whipped cream, for serving

1. Combine the cocoa, flour, sugar, and salt in a bowl. Stir in the milk. Drizzle in the butter and vanilla, and stir to combine. Stir in chocolate chips.

2. Spoon into a mason jar. Cover and store until needed, up to 1 day.

3. To serve, microwave for 45 seconds, until just set. Top with a dollop of whipped cream, if desired.

berry trifle

A friend served a version of this trifle while we were visiting her lake house, and I loved how colorful and flavorful it was. It's the perfect summer dessert when berries are at their peak. And with its patriotic colors, can't you just picture it on the menu for an Independence Day picnic?

JAR SIZE: half pint MAKES: 2 servings

4 ounces cream cheese at room temperature

½ cup whipping cream

2 tablespoons powdered sugar

1 teaspoon vanilla extract

1 cup cubed angel food cake or lady fingers

1 cup blueberries

1 cup raspberries

1. In a medium bowl, use a hand mixer at medium speed to beat the cream cheese just until smooth. Add the whipping cream and beat until fluffy, 2 to 3 minutes. Add the powdered sugar and vanilla, and beat until just combined.

2. To assemble, layer the cake, berries, and cream mixture in 2 layers. Cover and refrigerate until needed, up to 2 days. Serve chilled.

s'mores for two

I know this isn't much of a recipe, but I just love the idea of packing a little s'mores kit in a mason jar for a camping trip or bonfire. The glass will keep the marshmallows from getting smashed and the graham crackers from being crushed.

JAR SIZE: pint MAKES: 2 servings

1 (1.55-ounce) Hershey's milk chocolate bar, broken into 4 pieces

4 marshmallows

4 full sheets graham crackers, cracked in half

1. In 2 pint jars, divide the chocolate, marshmallows, and graham crackers. Store at room temperature until needed, up to 2 days.

2. Use skewers to toast the marshmallows over an open flame, then sandwich the marshmallow, along with a piece of chocolate, between two pieces of graham cracker.

no-bake blueberry cheesecake

These little cheesecakes don't need to go in the oven, which makes them an ideal treat for summer. In place of the blueberry compote, you could make a similar compote from fresh or frozen cherries, or you could even use a fruit pie filling.

JAR SIZE: half pint MAKES: 2 servings

¼ cup graham cracker crumbs
2 tablespoons melted butter
1 tablespoon brown sugar
6 ounces cream cheese, room temperature
3 tablespoons sweetened condensed milk
1 teaspoon vanilla extract
¼ cup light sour cream
1 tablespoon granulated sugar
½ cup blueberry compote (see note)

1. In a small bowl, combine the graham cracker crumbs with the butter and brown sugar until it resembles wet sand. Divide the mixture between 2 half-pint jars, and pack it into the bottom of the jars.

2. In a medium bowl, combine the cream cheese, sweetened condensed milk, and vanilla extract. Stir well with a spatula until the ingredients form a smooth mixture. Spoon into the jars on top of the crust.

3. Without rinsing the bowl, combine the sour cream and sugar. Stir until the sugar has dissolved. Spoon onto the custard in the jar. Divide the blueberry compote between the two jars. Cover and refrigerate until needed, up to 3 days.

Blueberry Compote: To make blueberry compote, combine 1 cup frozen blueberries and 1 teaspoon sugar in a small saucepan over medium-low heat. Simmer for 5 minutes until the blueberries soften and release their juices. Let cool completely before using. This will make around ¾ cup of compote; if you have extra, you can spoon it onto ice cream, yogurt, or pancakes.

bread pudding

I've seen plenty of cute recipes where bread pudding or cakes are baked in the oven right in a mason jar. But I'm just not willing to risk it—the glass used to make these jars isn't formulated to withstand the heat of an oven. But steam or boiling water is another story.... After all, that's how you can the jam and other preserved foods that these jars were originally intended for! It's essential to not skip the step of warming up the milk. It helps prevent thermal shock, which could cause the jars to break in the pot (trust me, I know from experience!).

JAR SIZE: half pint MAKES: 2 servings

¾ cup whole milk
1 egg
1 egg yolk
½ cup granulated sugar
1 teaspoon vanilla extract
½ teaspoon ground cinnamon
⅛ teaspoon kosher salt
3 slices raisin bread, cut into 1-inch cubes
2 tablespoons prepared caramel, for serving

1. Add about an inch of water to a tall stockpot and place a steamer rack in the bottom. Heat the water to a simmer.

2. Heat the milk in the microwave or in a small saucepan on the stove until very warm, 90°F to 100°F. In a small mixing bowl, whisk together the egg and yolk. Whisk in the sugar, vanilla, cinnamon, and salt, then slowly drizzle in the milk, whisking to combine. Divide the raisin bread between the jars and pour the milk mixture over the bread, using the back of a spoon to pack the bread into the jar as needed. Loosely screw two-part metal lids onto the jar, but don't tighten them. Put the jars on the steamer rack and put the lid on the pot. Adjust the heat to maintain a simmer and cook for 20 minutes.

3. With tongs or a silicone oven mitt, carefully remove the jars from the pot. Slowly open the lids (be careful, the contents might puff out when the pressure is released) and check for doneness: The milk mixture should be thick and custardy and the bread soft and spongy. Serve warm or at room temperature, drizzled with caramel.

lemon meringue jars

I couldn't write this chapter without including a variation on my very favorite dessert: lemon meringue pie! A few shortcuts—butter cookies and marshmallow fluff—stand in admirably for the crust and the meringue. If you don't have a culinary torch to brown the topping, it's still delicious untoasted.

JAR SIZE: half pint MAKES: 2 servings

1 egg

2 egg yolks

2 teaspoons lemon zest

½ cup sugar

¼ cup lemon juice (about 2 lemons)

1 tablespoon butter

6 butter cookies, such as Pepperidge Farm Chessmen

½ cup Marshmallow Fluff

1. Add an inch of water to the bottom of a double boiler and bring to a simmer over medium heat. Or, create a makeshift double boiler by nesting a metal or glass mixing bowl over a saucepan.

2. In a bowl, beat together the egg, egg yolk, lemon zest, and sugar until light and frothy. Add the lemon juice, then whisk to combine. Transfer the mixture to the top of the double boiler, reduce heat to maintain the simmer, and cook, stirring occasionally with the whisk, until the mixture thickens enough to coat the back of a spoon, about 10 minutes. Place a mesh strainer over a small bowl and pour the lemon curd through the strainer to strain out the zest and any bits of coagulated egg. Immediately stir in the butter. Let cool to room temperature.

3. To assemble jars, break up cookies into large chunks and add to each half-pint jar, putting 3 cookies in each jar. Spoon the cooled lemon curd over the cookies. Top each jar with ¼ cup Marshmallow Fluff. Optionally, use a culinary torch to lightly brown the marshmallow fluff. Serve immediately or refrigerate for up to 2 days.

strawberry shortcake jars

When we pick strawberries at a nearby farm, I always plan to make this quick and easy dessert. It's a fun treat to pack for a picnic or to serve on the porch after a dinner party. The prepared pound cakes that are found in the freezer case of your grocery store work well for this dessert, or you can bake one using your favorite recipe.

JAR SIZE: half pint MAKES: 2 servings

1 cup hulled and quartered strawberries
2¼ teaspoons granulated sugar, divided
1 tablespoon chopped fresh mint, plus whole mint leaves for garnish
½ cup whipping cream
½ teaspoon vanilla extract
1 cup cubed pound cake

1. Place the strawberries in a small mixing bowl. Sprinkle with ¼ teaspoon sugar and the mint, then toss to combine. Set aside.

2. In a medium mixing bowl, add the whipping cream, vanilla, and the remaining 2 teaspoons sugar. With a whisk or a hand mixer at medium to high speed, whisk to stiff peaks.

3. To assemble, layer the cake, berries, and whipped cream. Garnish with a mint leaf or two.

Note: To easily prep strawberries, gather the green hull between your thumb and forefinger. Holding the hull, use your other hand to slice it off. Turn the berry to sit on the cut end and slice it down the middle. If the pieces are still too big, give the berry a quarter turn and slice it again into quarters.

pistachio pudding parfaits

With its bright-green color, sweet cookie base, and airy whipped topping, this is a really fun kids' dessert.

JAR SIZE: half pint or smaller MAKES: 4 servings

1 (3.4-ounce) package instant pistachio pudding mix

16 Nilla Wafers

1 cup whipped topping, such as Cool Whip

2 tablespoons chopped pistachios

1. Make pudding according to package directions.

2. In a zip-top bag, crush the Nilla Wafers.

3. Divide the crushed cookies between the four jars. Spoon the pudding over the cookies, and top with a dollop of whipped topping over each. Garnish with the pistachios.

Common Conversions

1 gallon = 4 quarts = 8 pints = 16 cups = 128 fluid ounces = 3.8 liters

1 quart = 2 pints = 4 cups = 32 ounces = .95 liter

1 pint = 2 cups = 16 ounces = 480 ml

1 cup = 8 ounces = 240 ml

¼ cup = 4 tablespoons = 12 teaspoons = 2 ounces = 60 ml

1 tablespoon = 3 teaspoons = ½ fluid ounce = 15 ml

Temperature Conversions

Fahrenheit (°F)	Celsius (°C)
200°F	95°C
225°F	110°C
250°F	120°C
275°F	135°C
300°F	150°C
325°F	165°C
350°F	175°C
375°F	190°C
400°F	200°C
425°F	220°C
450°F	230°C
475°F	245°C

Volume Conversions

US	US equivalent	Metric
1 tablespoon (3 teaspoons)	½ fluid ounce	15 milliliters
¼ cup	2 fluid ounces	60 milliliters
⅓ cup	3 fluid ounces	90 milliliters
½ cup	4 fluid ounces	120 milliliters
⅔ cup	5 fluid ounces	150 milliliters
¾ cup	6 fluid ounces	180 milliliters
1 cup	8 fluid ounces	240 milliliters
2 cups	16 fluid ounces	480 milliliters

Weight Conversions

US	Metric
½ ounce	15 grams
1 ounce	30 grams
2 ounces	60 grams
¼ pound	115 grams
⅓ pound	150 grams
½ pound	225 grams
¾ pound	350 grams
1 pound	450 grams

Acknowledgments

Many thanks to Ball® Brand Fresh Preserving Products by Newell Brands for providing me with canning jars for recipe development and photography, many of which are featured in the photographs in this book. Check out https://www.freshpreserving.com to see their full selection of jars, lids, and accessories.

I'd also like to thank my fabulous photographer, Kelley Klein, of Kelley Klein Photography (www.kelleyklein.com). Her inspired eye, creativity, patience, and flexibility made our photo shoots fun.

Thank you, too, for the styling assistance of Jennifer Lazo, of Casa de Lazo, and Rachel Quartarone.

All of the beautiful photos in the book were shot on location in home kitchens in Atlanta. Kenzi Tainow, Claire Pearson, Chrissi Kallio, Jennifer Lazo, David and DeAnn Sinrich, and Aidy Restrepo: Thank you for graciously opening your homes to us so that we could use your lovely spaces as backdrops for my recipes.

About the Contributors

Jessica Goldbogen Harlan is a writer, recipe developer, cooking instructor, and caterer. Trained at the Institute of Culinary Education in New York City, she has developed a culinary philosophy that embraces simple but elegant flavor combinations, wholesome and seasonal ingredients, and uncomplicated methods. This is Jessica's eighth cookbook; other titles include *Ramen to the Rescue, Quinoa Cuisine* (cowritten with Kelley Sparwasser), and *Homemade Condiments.* She has also written for *Town & Country, Clean Eating,* About.com, and *Arthritis Today.* She lives in Atlanta with her husband, Chip, and her daughters, Sadie and Gillian.

Kelley Klein is a freelance photographer specializing in portrait and architectural photography. She received her BFA with a concentration in photography, as well as a BA in print journalism, from Georgia State University in 2005. Her work has been featured in numerous publications, including *The Atlanta Business Chronicle, Jezebel, Atlanta Journal-Constitution, The Huffington Post*, and HGTV.com. She currently lives in Atlanta with her husband, two daughters, two dogs, and a cat.